GOD, GOVERNMENT, GUNS...
A CHRISTIAN PERSPECTIVE

BY

GERALD DERSTINE

A GOSPEL CRUSADE Publication
Rt. 2, Box 279, Bradenton, Florida 34202

Dedicated to the glory of God, that we and future generations may always be blessed with the precious freedoms afforded us by this great land of the United States of America.

ACKNOWLEDGMENTS

Thanks to Angie Williams, Jeanie Strand, Phil and Joanne Derstine, Bob Armstrong and others who helped me in the writing and production of this book.

Special thanks to faithful friends and partners who undergird me with their prayers, giving me the courage to champion the cause of Christ.

God, Government, Guns . . .
A Christian Perspective

CONTENTS

INTRODUCTION

God, Government, Guns . . . A Christian Perspective

INTRODUCTION

Those familiar with my background and teaching through the years may find the title of this book shocking. Ordained as a Mennonite pastor in 1953, I was trained in non-political theology and embraced the conscientious objecter stand regarding military activity; therefore, I have always been quite sensitive to the issues discussed in this treatise.

However, in recent years I have encountered situations that prompted fresh research and, subsequently, more perfect understanding. This book is an attempt to explain to my fellow Americans, my Christian brethren — and my critics — my current beliefs on some controversial subjects.

Deep down in my heart I find myself neither Democrat nor Republican but *Christian* first, and next an American citizen concerned for the government of our country. I cast my vote for the individual adhering closest to Biblical principles, whether Democrat or Republican. My motivation is to promote Biblical God-oriented moral principles so the people of this country may enjoy our Creator's blessings. ''Righteousness exalteth a nation: but sin is a reproach to any people.'' Proverbs 14:34.

For years I found myself among the criticizers of our own country's lawmakers, including the President, shrugging them off as a pack of crooked politicians concerned only with money-making schemes and self-interests.

My thinking has been totally jarred by the staggering statistics relating to the legal deaths (murders) of unborn babies in our land. I have been humbled and ashamed before God that I had no interest in this matter during the early '70s when the abortion law was enacted. God, I feel, holds me equally responsible with my government for these innocent murdered babies — now numbering conservatively 20 million since this law went into effect.

You see, I thought by not being involved in the political system, by not voting, that I would be excused for the unGodly decisions made by our worldly politicians (lawmakers). However, through deep heart-searching on this matter, God has made me know that every American citizen is a part of the government of this country *and is equally responsible for its laws.*

I was naive and arrogant to think I would be excused from God's judgement for the sins of our country. I have learned that when God judges a nation for its sins, all people in the nation will share the consequences . . . the good and the bad. There is no doubt in my mind that our country will experience God's Divine judgement unless we repent. To repent means each of us American citizens must become active, both through prayer and physical involvement, informing our lawmakers what God has to say about moral issues affecting our nation.

We may think just one voice can accomplish very little in changing un-Godly laws; however, I will have to answer before God in the Judgement as to whether I attempted to obey His Word or merely ignore these critical issues.

In my study of this subject, I was astonished to find many Scriptures showing God's intense interest in the welfare of the peoples in various nations of the world. The following passage in Daniel 4:17, for example:

"This matter is by the decree of the watches, and the demand by the word of the holy ones: to the intent that the living may know that the most High ruleth in the kingdom of men, and giveth it to whomsoever he will, and setteth up over it the *basest* of men." (Nebuchadnezzar's condition before God dealt with him.)

The context indicates that Nebuchadnezzar was king by divine appointment. However, he was a base man in his despotic rule. The interpretation of his dream illustrated that Nebuchadnezzar was given his kingdom by God, but that God did hold the King personally responsible for what he did in his rule.

Four times in chapters 4 and 5 it is declared that the Most High rules in the kingdom of men, i.e., Daniel 4:17, 4:25, 4:32 and 5:21.

On the other hand, God also holds a people responsible for the government that is over them. 11 Chron. 7:14. "If my people which are called by my name, shall humble themselves, and pray, and seek my face, and turn from their wicked ways; then will I hear from heaven, and will forgive their sin, and will heal their land."

Note also in the life of Samuel that one man's prayer made the difference in an entire nation's victory over a formidable enemy. 1 Samuel 7:13, "So the Philistines were subdued, and they came no more into the coast of Israel: and the hand of the Lord was against the Philistines all the days of Samuel." Notice in 7:9...''Samuel cried unto the Lord for Israel and the Lord heard him. Israel's military battled the Philistines and ''the Lord thundered with a great thunder on that day'' and confused the enemy. One man's prayer turned the tide for a whole nation.

It appears our nation under President Reagan had a similar experience. God's people have been praying, and perhaps our President had a Divine leading when he gave orders to destroy the headquarters of the King of Terrorism in Libya. At this writing, our nation has been experiencing a time of rest and quietness from terrorism, at least from that nation. God never changes. He will honor the cry of his people and bless the nation that attempts to follow Divine leading.

My prayer is for our Christian citizens of America to seek God in earnest and consider their God-given responsibility regarding their role in Godly government. Our nation's founding fathers sought God for Divine direction in the making of our laws; the walls of many of the state capitols still reveal this as we find, in conspicuous places, Bible verses inscribed in marble or wood as a reminder that God was central in the making of this great nation.

My generation is held equally responsible to retain Godly principles for our children and future generations. This book is a token effort to affect the hearts and minds of responsible people to help restore Godliness once again to an apathetic, immoral people plagued with devastating evil habits, drugs, alcohol, rebellion and wickedness.

I am aware that the material contained in the following pages will not be popular with everyone, and some well-meaning people may disagree with my stands on these issues. The book is not intended as an exhaustive study; it's merely an attempt to provoke our thinking and prod us toward action in restoring Godly government.

CHAPTER 1

Why Should Christians Be Concerned About Political Issues?

As citizens of the United States of America, we have the privilege to vote for the president and government leaders of our choice.

Inasmuch as we are considered by our heritage to be a ''Christian nation,'' I believe that every Christian should have an interest in the political system. It is through the political system that we form our laws and our regulations for our families and other citizens of this country. As a Christian, I believe it is our *responsibility* to speak for the right things which we have gleaned from the Bible, in relation to current laws for our land. I feel that Christians need to be involved in the political system since this is where the laws for governing our people evolve. ''Righteousness exalteth a nation: but sin is a reproach to any people.'' Prov. 14:13

On the other hand, we understand the secular system and make a place for it in our society. To respect the individual rights of all people our laws allow pluralism of belief, and even protect the rights of unbelievers or atheists.

However, the purpose of law is to set guidelines for peoples' lifestyle and surely every Christian should desire each of our laws to be God-blessed and God-honoring. The secular world cannot possibly make God-honoring laws if they are not God-fearing. The church has that mandate. Prov. 2:9.

Church, we still have these rights in America. Once the law is made, we are required to honor it; however, in our system we

1

have the privilege to make changes. . . thus we have the varied political parties.

I am convinced that our present administration has been attempting to honor Godly, Bible-based rulings. Examples are public stands taken on the abortion issue, prayer and Bible reading in public institutions, encouraging higher age for alcoholic beverage consumption, upholding Judaeo-Christian, Moses law-oriented capital punishment rulings to maintain law and order in a secular world, and others. This administration values counsel from Christian and Jewish leaders. I have personally been involved several times in White House briefings regarding sensitive issues.

CHAPTER 2

Some of Your Critics Believe In Total Separation of Church and State. How Do You Feel About That?

I have personally been brought up this way. Historically, the church in which I was ordained had a very strong stand that church and state should be totally separated. We were separated to the extent that we were discouraged even from voting. We detached ourselves from the secular society, the political system or government process.

However, in recent years, I have begun to see things more realistically. I've watched our secular system pass laws that permit people to murder unborn babies -- taking the life of individuals, which I know is against the Word of God. That is one of the issues that has awakened me to the fact that Christians should be involved in the political process, in law-making.

I believe in prayer as part of the process. But I believe that when one prays he will also take action in the direction of that which he is praying for and become involved. My background tended to isolate me from the political process, and many people who take the historical stand of my church assume they are uninvolved.

Yet I find them in peace movements, becoming quite vocal against our present governmental system, inadvertently helping to water down our Christian principles. By coming against a president who is attempting to retain and restore Biblical principles, we find ourselves ''activists'' in a negative sense though we say we are neutral. Eccl. 8:2,4.

I believe there should be a definite involvement both in praying and in a vocal way, standing up for the leader of your nation who was placed there by God, particularly a leader who professes to honor Biblical principles. We need to back our leaders so that we as a nation will be an example of Godly principles to the rest of the nations of the world. The Apostle Paul admonished Titus, "Put them in mind to be subject to principalities and powers, to obey magistrates, to be ready to every good work." Titus 3:1

CHAPTER 3

Should Christians Remain Neutral And Refrain From Taking A Stand For One Side Or The Other?

No, I believe that is a mistake. Those who live under a dictatorship or totalitarian style of government know from the onset that their vote will have no effect on the outcome of the election, and they have no voice in the making of their government's laws and rules.

However, with the freedoms we have in the United States, I believe we are responsible before God if we are to retain Christian concepts in the rulership of our land. It is up to Bible-believing people to exercise the privilege they have as U.S. citizens to take a stand and share their Scriptural understanding of the Christian concepts that will shape our laws and rules.

When people choose to take a neutral stance or no stand at all, they still make a statement because by their silence they are aiding those who are speaking. Luke 11:23. A Democratic nation is governed by those who let their voice be heard. Silence puts more power in the hands of those who are speaking.

From my viewpoint, if a person says he is deliberately taking a neutral stand, I believe that, unknowingly, he becomes irresponsible. Indirectly, he is aiding the enemy of our country -- primarily because the nations of this world are secular; they require the law to control them.

God has given the Ten Commandments from the Old Testament to regulate the actions of people according to the law of Moses. We have the law for the secular world that does not know or perhaps honor God, thus we have a means by which the world can measure itself and maintain a semblance of order.

I am a Christian, but I am also an American citizen. As an American citizen, I have a right and responsibility to uphold or disagree with the laws of my country. Since I am a Christian who also belongs to the Kingdom of God, I have the Kingdom of God to consider as well. . . and that is based on the Bible, patterned after the lifestyle of Jesus Christ. Read Matthew 5:1-16

As a Christian citizen in a secular world, I strive to utilize my freedom to inject my Godly influence and faith into a secular system. I know that a secular system will not understand the Beatitudes. They will not be able to adhere to ''the grace message.'' They don't have the ability to exercise grace, so only the Christian community can do this.

I see two communities -- the secular community and the Christian community. The Christian community has its own laws to abide by, the Kingdom of God principles which are higher than the world standards. We need to administer those Kingdom of God principles as much as possible into the secular world system, hoping and praying for the secular world system to be influenced by the kingdom of God.

The secular world system has secular-minded leaders, so we must use secular principles of which the best we have is the law.

As a Christian, I understand the Christian principles of grace and peace.

From that standpoint, I feel Christians are wrong when they say, ''My neutral stand is the way God wants it to be.'' I believe that is heresy, and that it is wrong. If you consistently remain neutral, then perhaps you fall into the category of the old saying, ''You are so spiritually-minded, that you're no earthly good.''

If we are going to be heavenly-minded people who do good on this earth, we must take an active role in speaking up concerning government issues, not merely in a negative sense, like disagreeing with your government, but also in a *positive* sense. Administer assistance to the government through involvement, whether vocal or written.

A Christian might also become a part of the government system in order to inject influence from within. As God's representatives we desire to change the evils of the secular society through our living influence. As Christians we are responsible to demonstrate God's way and God's love to the world. God does still love the world. John 3:16. And His desire is that the world would turn from their wicked ways and look to God. We are God's representatives to effect this change.

Total uninvolvement certainly speaks a message to the enemy of your country because then they may assume you are a sympathizer, thereby aiding their cause, and thus assist their overthrowing of your democratic privileges.

Remember, our democratic ordinances state we are a government of the people, for the people and by the people of our nation. Only according to people's involvement will we have government, and only the type of people, Christian or secular, will determine the type of government and its laws. Christians in America have a serious responsibility if they intend to retain their liberty and freedom.

I am grateful to live in a nation such as ours where we can enjoy the freedoms based on the convictions of our Godly forefathers who sought Divine direction. I, in turn, have committed myself to give input that will help retain our rights and Godly principles.

"The hottest places in Hell are reserved for those who, in a period of moral crisis, maintain their neutrality." -Dante

How Do You Interpret The Portion Of Scripture Where Jesus Was Asked About Payment Of Taxes, And Said You Must Render Unto Caesar That Which Is Caesar's And To God That Which Is God's? Does This Infer That Christians Should Not Get Involved In Government Affairs?

Then Jesus answered and said to them, ''Render to Caesar the things that are Caesar's, and to God the things that are God's.'' And they marveled at Him. Mark 12:17 and Matt. 17:24-27.

We pay taxes so our government can maintain our society with proper order. God gave us the Ten Commandments, the Law, for that purpose — to maintain order. The law, including capital punishment — an eye for an eye, a tooth for a tooth — is for people who do not respect God's love and peace and *will only respond to force or power.* When they observe government has power and authority, this becomes a deterrant to the individual who wants his own way at the expense of others or is unable to control his actions.

Control comes by enforcing the law. The maintenance of law and order is a *divine institution* from God. Government for secular society is a divine institution. Though we are Christian, we are still part of society in this world and responsible to uphold law and order.

When God's Word says that we should pray for those in authority, He also intends that we render unto Caesar that which is Caesar's. He also intends that we pay our taxes; he demands our support, our help; especially toward a government that is attempting to follow the pattern of God according to the Holy Scriptures. Part of our problem in America, where we have a free democratic form of government, is that we have differences of interpretation regarding various Scripture portions. Certain men's interpretations of the Scriptures will not permit a Christian to participate in the political system, leaving it totally to secular society. However, without the Godly influence of Bible-believing Christians, our government will slip further and further away from its Bible-based roots. Secular government leaders without faith in God cannot possibly design Bibically based laws or statutes.

I believe the Christian is responsible to pay the government taxes when he knows he has a Divine mandate to render unto Caesar that which belongs to Caesar. Through obedience to our government we maintain hope to retain liberty and freedom to serve God.

I also feel it is wrong to withhold portions of our taxes owed to our government because of our objection to certain laws or rulings our government holds. If Christians practiced this, then others would follow suit for reasons of their own and great confusion would result.

We are not held accountable in God's sight for how every penny is spent by Caesar. In obedience I render to Caesar that which Caesar demands and to God what God demands. May we trust God and walk in obedience to Him. Pray that you are not directed by a spirit of rebellion. Romans 13:5,6 — ''wherefore ye must needs be subject, not only for wrath, but also for conscience sake. For this cause pay ye taxes also: for they are God's ministers, attending continually upon this very thing.''

CHAPTER 5

How Did Our Forefathers Want Our Nation To Be?

The Constitution of our United States, upon its formation, was bathed in serious prayer. The Pledge of Allegiance to our flag states we are ''a republic under God,'' and that we are also a democracy. Basically, the aspect of being a republic under God is paramount . . . ''one nation, indivisible, with liberty and justice for all.''

We are a republic first; we are a democracy second. Our forefathers carefully worded that document, knowing that a democracy with the blessings that they anticipated could never become fulfilled without the will of God in all the laws that this nation embraced.

Democracy infers the idea that everyone has a voice in formulating the laws of our land. If everyone has this right, and yet does not respect God or have any fear of God, you may be sure we will have chaos. A democracy will not function with freedom and justice for all individuals without God in its center.

Our founding fathers, who held deep religious convictions, were careful to make us aware that we are first of all a republic, an independent nation under God, but yet made up of people with individual rights to help make that nation function. In our early days, that's what made America great. That is what will make our nation continue to be great. People need to respect God and look to Him as their source of answers to world problems.''When the righteous are in authority, the people rejoice; but when the wicked beareth rule, the people mourn.'' Prov. 29:2.

The answers to these problems lie between the two covers of our Bible. This was very clearly stated by our President Ronald Reagan in 1982, when he brought to the attention of the American people and the world the need to recognize the value of Bible reading to retain Godly principles... ''The Year of the Bible.'' I think it is commendable also on his part to recognize the year of 1987 as ''A Year of Thanksgiving!''

CHAPTER 6

Why Do You Seem To Single Out Communism As Something So Evil?

My answer to that question requires an understanding of those who originated the teaching or theology of modern-day Communism.

Both Mr. Lenin and Karl Marx very openly stated their unbelief in a personal living Creator God. Furthermore, their teachings advocate removing from the minds of men the very thoughts and ideology found written in the inspired Holy Scriptures. These men are admitted atheists, not recognizing the existence of God.

How could any righteous, God-honoring semblence of government be established upon this earth with leadership adhering to anti-Christ, anti-God principles? History shows us that all nations accepting this form of government ultimately enslave their peoples. We had the Bamboo Curtain, the Iron Curtain, the Berlin wall and all kinds of rigid rulings and laws designed to force the peoples under this rigid Godless ideology to remain in their land.

Some well-meaning Christians deceive themselves into thinking that by being sympathetic toward anti-God Communism we can ultimately cause them to believe in our Christ. Indeed, let us pray for them and believe for their salvation, but we cannot support in any way their fundamental denial of God as a life-changing force. Communism is anti-God and the fruit of Communism bears this out. Jesus said, "By their fruits ye shall know them." Matt. 7:20.

Some people are so anxious for positive change that they fall for any new or different thing. Individuals pursuing intellectual explanations easily depart from faith in God. Intellectual reasoning will satisfy at least temporarily the self or ego. It demands no self-denial but rather self-gratification. You will find the seed-bed for Communism is found in our institutions of learning — universities, colleges, seminaries and the like. Socialistic logic at first sounds very proper to lift up mankind from his earthly misfortunes. Humanistic logic makes great sense to the intellectual mind that is void of God's Word.

To move in total liberty and freedom upon this earth is to know the Truth. Jesus Christ said, "I am the way, the truth and the life". . . John 14:6. "And ye shall know the truth, and the truth shall make you free." John 8:32. Faith in God yields Godly fruit.

Why should a Christian even consider reading any literature written by anti-God authors such as Karl Marx or Lenin or any of their sympathizers unless he is already doubting the reality of God? The Bible has the total answer to our world's problems. People have only to follow its great truths.

Liberation theology is also a direct result of unbelief in the Divine inspiration of the Holy Scriptures. Our weak faith lends credibility to compromise. A weak Christian may entertain the notion that if we mix some of Marx along with the Bible, perhaps we will have peace in the world. Yes, you will have peace at the cost of diluting God and His principles from your mind and heart. You will end up with atheists or God-haters as your government leaders, and Christians will be among the first to suffer at their hands.

The Holy Spirit makes us sensitive to His Divine Will; therefore, cautious in lending support to any movement related to Communistic ideologies. Flee from them.

A more complete answer to this question is contained in the following excerpt from *America, Wake Up*, by Bill and Nita Scoggan.

In 1924, Lenin said: "First we will take over eastern Europe, second the masses of Asia, then we will surround America." — the last bastion of freedom. "We will not have to fight. It will fall into our hands like overripe fruit."

Many today are saying Better Red Than Dead. Are we willing to trade our liberty for a little temporary safety?

Secretary of Defense Caspar Weinberger said, "I don't subscribe to the Better Red Than Dead philosophy. How can people live in a slave society which monitors every word that's said and doesn't permit them freedom of expression, freedom of religion — and will consign them to a concentration camp or a slave labor camp?"

Patrick Henry put it very plainly, "Is life so sweet and peace so dear, as to be purchased for the price of chains?"

Behind the smiles and detente lie the Communist goals of world conquest. What have we learned from Romania, Korea, Viet Nam, Cambodia, Poland and Afghanistan? The price of liberty is the ability to defend and preserve it.

We need to remember what the Communists have written about their aims: "Let the ruling classes tremble at a Communist revolution. The proletarians have nothing to lose but their chains. They have a world to win." (The Communist Manifesto)

They have not been secretive about their views and aims for world conquest.

Carl Marx said the Communist aims were to:

1. De-throne God.
2. Destroy capitalism.
3. Abolish private property.
4. Eliminate the family.

Communist goals haven't changed.

When Kruschev came to America in the 1950's and spoke to the United Nations, he took off his shoe and pounded it on the lectern to emphasize his point when he said of the United States: "We'll bury you!" He said that on American television. Millions heard it, but didn't believe it.

Millions of Americans today have had a lapse in memory, and have forgotten the Communist goals for world control.

Communists are always working toward their goals of world conquest. They are very patient. They are not concerned if it doesn't happen this year, or next year. They keep hammering away at a nation. They will try many tactics . . . infiltration, terrorism, propaganda, attack on the government, weakening the economy, racial strife, and civil unrest.

Communists work hard to sway and change world opinion, so the world will view the Communists as fighting for the workers, fighting for the minorities, fighting to better those under imperialism and capitalism — namely the United States. One has only to look at the people risking their lives to escape from behind the Iron Curtain, the Berlin Wall, or the slave labor camps to see the life they offer their own people.

Soviet propaganda portrays Communists as ''peace loving'' — not as aggressors working to take over countries such as Afghanistan, South Africa and Mexico. Already many nations like Ethiopa — whose Christian leader, Haile Selasie, mysteriously disappeared — have been overturned and are under Communist rule. Brutality and famine have taken the lives of thousands of people who are not allowed to leave the drought-stricken area. Eventually these ''peace-loving'' Communists plan to defeat America and take over the world.

The World War 1 hero, Alvin York, said in 1941: ''The thing people forget is that freedom is so precious we don't just fight for it once and stop.''

Chapter 7

What Can People Do To Help The Oppressed People, Besides Voting And Praying?

We can send teams to different countries with humanitarian aid and Bible teaching teams. My burden is to share the principles of the Kingdom of God to Christian believers around the world. The teachings of Jesus Christ are truth and light. Light replaces darkness. Light is the more dominant force. Darkness is merely the absence of light. John 8:12.

Many Christians are extremely shallow in their understanding of God, thus are vulnerable to doubt and unbelief. I am attempting through our "Kingdom Living Institute," a four-week leadership training program, to shore up the faith and courage of the church in our Latin American nations.

I send American pastors from active local churches to teach alongside national pastors of these Spanish nations. Their faith is sharpened and the Light shines brighter. My goal is to place at least three Video Schools in each Spanish-speaking nation of the world. . . directed by a qualified leader of that nation. We must be careful not to become politically-oriented in our aid to the oppressed peoples of foreign governments. We may disagree with some of our government's policies, but surely have no Godly-Biblical right to champion our disfavor alongside the peoples of the foreign governments.

Some conservative churches who were against American involvement in Vietnam continued to send support after the war was over, sharing various types of aid, implying their disfavor of our government's involvement. My feeling is that the church should always be quick to assist the hurting, and slow to criticize and condemn. God has called us to preach the ''Good News'' of a free salvation that all may know Him! John 3:16-17.

CHAPTER 8

Should People In Communist Countries Be Encouraged To Rebel Against Their Government, Or Should They Trust God? How Militant And Active Should Christians Be In Pursuing Godly Leadership For Their Country?

A Christian community in this world has a mandate from God to pray and anticipate a change of government . . . in whatever way God chooses to bring that change about. He could raise up an activist that's a Spirit-filled Christian, a Moses, a writer of books. In Russia they have people who are writing books and writing songs that challenge their present anti-God system. We are to utilize any liberty available to influence a repressive anti-God government without blatantly breaking moral laws.

In spite of extreme religous repression, there are four Christians in Russia for every one member of the Communist party, according to sources quoted by noted historian Dr. Vinson Synan. He believes, and I agree, that the concentrated prayers of Christians can cause a confrontation between the powers of darkness and the power of the Holy Spirit — and the light of Jesus Christ can bring about a miraculous change.

I think it is out of order for Christians to be totally naive and dormant and just say, "Whatever happens is supposed to happen" and "God's will be done." This world will never be changed that way!

God has given us a mandate through Jesus Christ to pray that the Kingdom of God come . . . ''Thy kingdom come, Thy will be done in earth as it is in heaven.''Matthew 6:9,10. I think we should utilize every means possible in a non-violent manner to influence anti-God laws by means of letters, telephone calls, speeches, songs and personal contacts with those in authority. The Christian's personal witness to the sinner also accomplishes this. Every Christian should be an activist toward the Kingdom of God. What we are doing in the United States right now is trying to maintain and retain Kingdom of God principles . . . His righteousness, peace and joy.

CHAPTER 9

Is Capitalism An Evil In Our World?

My critics say that "capitalism" is a bad influence in our world. They say the United States is "filthy rich" and only the rich people share the blessings, that the poor people in our country have no place or say anymore. . . it is only theoretical that the poor have a voice . . . the rich are controlling everything. Therefore they lobby for a change in our present form of government, thinking socialism or perhaps even communism may be a viable alternative.

I believe they are misguided.

I think it is very destructive for individuals to focus on our country's faults. They say,"We need a revolution. We need change." Rather, we need to set an example by our lifestyle, and build on those things that are right about our country. Presently, we have freedom to speak, enabling us to improve the evils that exist. But to take the attitude that we are so bad that we should consider a socialistic form of government takes us a big step toward totalitarian anti-God Communism.

We have the promise in the Scripture that the poor will always be with us. Some misinformed Christians think that the rich are to be avoided. But in the Scriptures we can see that Jesus ministered to both the poor and the prosperous. Nicodemus, for example, John 3:1. Jesus made great efforts to reach the rich people.

Zaccheus was a rich man, a tax collector. When Jesus looked up at that wealthy man in the tree, He called for Zaccheus to come down. "I'm going to your house for dinner," Jesus said. Now that could be viewed as discrimination by some people because He chose to turn His back on the poor and socialize with a rich man.

God has blessed and prospered us because of the Godly values our nation was founded upon. We must remember that He has blessed us with abundance so that we may give to others who have needs.

CHAPTER 10

At What Point Do You Think We Should Support Our Country's Military Intervention In Other Governments' Affairs?

I feel we are responsible to back up our President whom we pray for and whom we duly elected to lead us as a secular nation. To do otherwise is to create division and confusion, leaving us in a weak and vulnerable condition. I believe we have a Godly mandate to help our president fulfill what he was elected to do — to lead us. It is our duty to pray that he makes wise decisions, based on knowledgable counsel he receives and Divine direction from God.

I believe our president attempts to seek the mind of God. Our current president, Ronald Reagan, has consistently asked for Christian leaders and ministers to come to the White House to give counsel on all the major issues that relate to our nation. He accepts counsel from God's prophets. If he feels directed to send military intervention, I believe it is the duty of the Church to back him up and pray for him to fulfill what he needs to do.

To clarify this reasoning, one needs to understand the difference between fulfilling the responsibility of serving a secular nation and serving the church.

In heaven there will be no wars because there is no devil. In this world there will be wars because the devil is the prince and power of the air. Once Christ returns and removes the powers of Satan, there will be no more wars . . . there will be no more secular nations. There will be no enemy who is anti-God. However, God still uses Moses' law to control the negative powers in our world.

There are two kingdoms that the Christian interacts with — the kingdom of this world, which is the secular nation, and the Kingdom of God which is the spiritual nation that the Body of Christ, the church, relates to. Christians have the unique dynamics of expression within a spiritual kingdom, as well as relating to an earthly, natural, secular kingdom. So they are to govern their lifestyle under the Kingdom of God, and yet they must relate and live in the world's secular system.

What Spirit-filled Christian people need to understand is that although we are spiritual, we are also secular, or natural too. We must eat food, sleep, work for a living. If we use buildings we must have buildings on property that belongs to this world. This world is under a curse destined to be damned, burned up and destroyed.

Christians need to understand that if we are going to help this society, we must involve ourselves to the best of our ability, and through our convictions, influence the government that invites our participation.

Look at Russia. The communist government does not believe in God. Christians who live there don't have a voice in their government. Most of their services and meetings are held in secret. Communist, Marxist governments cannot tolerate Godly freedoms.

Christians suppressed by these governments may never have religious freedom here on earth. However, they may still be blessed of God if they choose to seek Him and pray. This blessing will be manifested in ways other than the material blessings and individual freedoms we enjoy in a free nation such as the United States. Christians living under oppression should continue to pray for their government leaders, looking to God to intervene in some way. Prayer *can* change things!

CHAPTER 11

What Is Your Position On The "Peace Issue"?

I believe that peace organizations, in general, are sincere and well-meaning, but their vision is short-ranged. They don't look down the path very far. They look at the present state of affairs and think that by not getting involved we won't see any more bullets flying. Their feeling is, negotiate with the enemy . . . attempt to avoid conflict. That is idealistic, however; quite unrealistic!

It may be realistic if only Christians were involved; Christians understand the concept of preferring the other before one's self. But the unsaved man that's bent on destruction and wants to change the world into a total secular system has an unregenerate heart. He will not nor cannot respond to the golden rule, ''Do unto others as ye would have them do unto you.''

I see the church as another entity. The church operates in the Kingdom of God; the church is the people of God. As church people living in a secular nation, we have to understand the secular view and its response to conflict and the enemy. The secular world is void of faith in God, and thusly, responds to the question of peace using the earthly tools of military and diplomacy.

I feel justified to encourage leaders of our government, as far as my convictions allow me, to give aid to people of like mind who are being oppressed. I'm not suggesting we should give military aid in every case. But I believe that Christians need to assist and help those oppressed suffering people in the nations friendly to our government, particularly in our hemisphere.

24

The people of Nicaragua are repressed, oppressed, and deceived by a false power that has promised democracy. Today they are being forced to learn Marxism, a communistic ideology, against their will. This is not democracy or freedom. The majority of Nicaraguan people reject this system. As their democratic freedom-loving neighbors we have a responsibility to come to their aid and assist them in regaining their freedom.

Our first responsibility is to pray for them. We also assist those who have fled their homeland, seeking refuge in neighboring free countries. I believe the United States has a responsibility to defend its past promise to defend the smaller nations on our hemisphere from foreign domination through a treaty known as the Monroe Doctrine.

Communist governments often use peace organizations as fronts to spread propaganda that furthers their own cause. I have personally met and spoken with peace movement advocates who have softened on their Christian beliefs and openly say Communism is not so bad . . . that perhaps our country is ready for change . . a renaissance is in the making. They wish to avoid war at any cost and are willing to dilute their own Godly ideals to pacify the enemy. They are quick to say God is against war when actually we see in the Bible that God often disciplined wicked unregenerate people and nations with war.

God is against Satan who deceives and controls people's minds. War, or the threat of war, is used by God as a deterrent against Satan's works in the minds of men. A recent example was our President's decision to use military action against the irrational, unGodly, terrorist-oriented Kadafy of Libya. This aggressive act of war seems to have discouraged his terrorist tactics throughout the world — at least for several months at this writing. Israel understands this principle. This is what Moses' law is all about. As the kingdom of this world practices the old law of ''an eye for an eye,'' the church has the opportunity to demonstrate and declare the *true peace message* of Jesus Christ as Saviour and Messiah to the world.

CHAPTER 12

Would You Allow Your Children To Go To War? What Do You Tell Young People In Your Church?

As a leader in the church, I must promote peace. My Mennonite upbringing and training, which advocates nonresistance or pacifism, has formed my personal belief in the "conscientious objector" ideology. I feel we should teach our young people the principles of the Sermon on the Mount . . . the Beatitudes.

We should encourage our children to be obedient and wait upon the Lord. Each individual's convictions should be a personal matter. My personal convictions would not allow me to enter the military and train to kill someone. On the other hand, I have no right to demand that my fellow Christians   adhere to my conviction in this matter but rather allow the Holy Spirit to direct their own leading. 1 Peter 5:3. I need to understand that God must have a voice also in the military segment of our national government.

During the earlier years of draft conscription I would write letters to our governmental authorities requesting "conscientious objector" status for our youth. They would then serve their time in "alternate service," as hospital aides or other social service volunteers. In some cases, they would go into the armed forces in a "non-combatant" role, such as a medic.

I still encourage people — including my own children — to be a "conscientious objector." But, if my children desired or felt obligated to serve in the armed forces, I would allow it to be their own individual decision — and give them my blessing.

1 Cor. 8:11-13.

I honor those who have risked and given their lives for the sake of our nation's democracy and freedom. And I praise God for Christian men and women who uphold their faith in God while serving in the armed forces. I believe it is wrong for a church to demand that their youth comply with the conviction of the leaders of the church. That type of action makes the organized church a god in the place of our true heavenly Father. We are individually to be led and directed by His Holy Spirit. 1 John 2:27, 1 Peter 5:3.

Genuine Christianity gives every Christian individual the right to follow the direction and leading of the Holy Spirit as it comes through his own conscience and the way he interprets the Word of God. I believe it is right for leaders of the church to interpret the Word of God the way they see it; and teach it that way to their congregations, yet giving the Holy Spirit His right to instill conviction and direction.

Therefore, we may have conscientious objectors and non-conscientious objectors in the same church. This should not affect your relationship with God.

CHAPTER 13

Should We As Peace-Loving Christians Support The Nuclear Freeze?

No. As long as the Communist government leaders of Russia and her allies with their anti-God ideology, have never retracted their aggressive statement of their ultimate plans to conquer the world, then I think it is wrong for us to support any movement that calls for a nuclear freeze.

It is difficult for me to believe that our enemies, as long as they voice this goal, would keep any promise to curtail their aggression. We know that nuclear war could destroy the lives of millions of people. If that power is put only into the hands of an enemy, he may use that form of power or whatever other form is necessary to control the minds of the *entire* human race.

For me as a Christian, my first love is God. I believe in God. I would rather die for my faith than have to give in to an ungodly government and be forced to deny God. That's why I am not fearful of nuclear holocaust. My fear of God is greater.

The only reason enemy nations who are anti-Christ refrain from using their nuclear power against us is because our own country has more than enough of that same power with which to retaliate, thus acting as a deterrent. Of course, there is always a danger of this power being abused by an irrational, temperamental or careless leader in our own country or any other country. The threat of nuclear war is real, but I feel it is wrong for us to resist our own government in this matter so closely related to safeguarding our freedoms.

CHAPTER 14

Do You Think Christians Should Support Our Own Government Policy On Maintaining The Arms Race?

We are stockpiling arms, and it seems to have become a "chess game" of who has the most powerful arsenal. In the natural this is frightening, but I feel it has become a necessary policy.

I'm in favor of our country doing what is necessary to act as a deterrent against the enemy overruning us or other free nations. Not to accelerate the race, but to assure a "balance." I feel it is necessary for our country to be sufficiently equipped to deal with any enemy anti-God nation.

In the secular world, a strong military position provides one of strength for negotiation and diplomacy. However, we as Christians realize that military strength alone is not enough. We need God's blessing, and that comes with the concerted prayers of Godly people. A nation blessed of God will be a powerful one, with or without the greatest military strength. Israel is a good example of this.

I certainly do support the recent effort that is being made to reduce the arsenal. Negotiation in that sense, I believe, is extremely valuable. It is essential that government leaders of the world make every effort to keep talking with each other . . . to keep communications open in an effort towards peace and understanding. It is in communication where the Spirit has a chance to come through. However, I'm for our government negotiating from a *position of strength*!

Nations with un-Godly ideals resort to Leninism, Marxism, and Communism. These ideologies promote military states with leaders who seem to respect only the physical power aspect . . . I believe our President understands this, and accordingly sees the need to keep our military strong.

CHAPTER 15

How Can A Soldier In Combat Be A True Christian?

First of all, that person apparently sensed a personal call and conviction to be a part of the military as a Christian. Or perhaps he may have found Jesus Christ as Saviour and Lord while serving in the military.

Many soldiers have given testimony of their finding Christ on the battlefields of war. Instantly such a soldier becomes the temple of God with Christ in his heart. Romans 10:9.

The soldier receives his strength and guidance from the same source as any civilian Christian. The soldier prays and reads the Holy Scripture for his spiritual strength and maturity and attends chapel services along with other fellow Christian soldiers whenever possible.

I have personally spoken to military personnel including soldiers who have exciting testimonies of God's special leading and protection for their lives, especially in battle. Prayer to God is very intense for soldiers during times of battle.

Incredible stories of God guiding certain of our American Generals during World War 11 have helped convince me that God does not forsake men or lend a deaf ear to their prayers for Divine guidance. A personal friend to the late General and former President Eisenhower related to me how General Eisenhower prayed to God for wisdom and guidance and credited God for his success in fulfilling victory on the battlefield.

A Christian soldier is keenly aware of his responsibility to perform the duties assigned him by his superiors, to honor the laws upheld by his government.

In keeping with that, I believe that a Christian who has made the decision to serve in our country's armed forces should be obedient to those in authority over him — and not worry over whether the enemy he confronts may be a Christian who is carrying out orders assigned by an opposing government. 1 Peter 2:13

In our U.S. government we have a choice for alternate service; however, in totalitarian governments there is no choice. The only way our type of government may continue to exist is to defend it with men of Godly moral principles. I believe Christians with fervent faith in God are very important in our military system.

CHAPTER 16

What Does "Conservative" Vs. "Liberal," Or Republican Or Democrat Have To Do With Christianity?

The differences in these terms or labels became sharply defined during the last election when the Democratic platform endorsed liberal views on abortion rights, the Equal Rights Amendment, keeping prayer and Bible reading out of the schools — everything most born-again Christians would be against.

The Republicans, on the other hand, clearly demonstrated that they favored the conservative Christian perspective on the issues of abortion, prayer and Bible reading in our public schools, etc. Their platform was very obviously more Judeo-Christian oriented, causing the evangelical born-again Christian to take note and become involved in the voting process. Our President actually wrote a book revealing the evils of abortion. Many Christians felt it mandatory to side with the party espousing the Christian Godly moral issues to spare our country from the Humanism of unGodly ideology, and thus God's judgement.

However, the lines are not always that clearly drawn, and I believe there will be some modifications in the next election. I think a Christian can be a Democrat, a Republican, an Independent, or whatever. What causes a Christian to respond are the issues, the moral and Biblical issues, in particular, those pertaining to lifestyle.

How can we call ourselves Christians when we approve the

slaughter of unborn babies, or do not allow prayer in our public schools, while at the same time prayer is permitted in our Congress?

As I watched the Congressional channel on cable television, I was amazed at the long, fervent prayer that was offered just before Congress went into session. I thought, ''Praise God!'' Yet the very men who were allowing this prayer display discrimination and irresponsibility by saying it's wrong for our children to have prayer in their classrooms. Some parents don't want their children exposed to God. I believe Christians should be strong in their conviction and say, ''We know our history. We have been blessed as a nation because we have kept God in our nation!'' There is one God and He is Lord.

In summary, *Conservative,* in my view, means to adhere to the Biblical principles and concepts our founding forefathers believed in when they formed the United States Constitution and Bill of Rights. To be *Liberal* means allowing our principles to be changed according to the ideas and feelings of the majority of the people who understand issues their way, whether it leans toward Biblical morality or not. Generally, the liberal mind embraces Humanism and does not esteem the Bible or the Word of God to be important in their philosophy of life.

CHAPTER 17

What Is Your Stand Regarding Christians Accepting "Liberation Theology"?

To accept "Liberation Theology" or "Process Theology" is to deny Jesus Christ as Lord. This ideology has crept into the minds of sincere well-meaning Christian leaders. Certainly it falls in the category of deception and compromise. The compromise is to exchange the Lordship of one absolute God with His Holy Word for a program of social reform through sympathetic human efforts.

January 27, 1984, the Don Bell Report defined liberation theology this way..."Salvation is transformed into political liberation. Repentance becomes denunciation of the status quo. The Holy Spirit is replaced by the human spirit. The church becomes the world community. Conversion is translated into social action. Liberation theology is communism in Christian clothing."

Liberation Theology is now being promoted by many churches in the National Council of Churches, particularly in Latin America. It uses traditional theological terms but changes their meaning. The goal of the church becomes the improvement of the physical well-being of people, particularly poor people. Jesus is portrayed as a revolutionary agitator seeking to overthrow the offensive government authorities. Therefore anyone who is seeking to overthrow existing authority tends to be sanctioned.

According to liberation theology, sin is the oppression practiced by the government, and righteousness consists of activities which aim to overthrow the government. It is also permissible to use violence in pursuit of this revolutionary goal. Thus liberation theology justifies and promotes violent revolution, and prepares the way for an alliance with anti-God Communists.

November 15, 1984, John F. McManus in his syndicated column, stated... "Boiled down to its essence, liberation theology is the re-interpretation of Christianity according to the concepts of Marxism. Those who follow its lead start with the ideology of Marx and then seek to reshape Holy Scripture to agree with it. Marx, of course espoused materialism which regards matter as the world's reality. He rejected all belief in anything spiritual, including God, man's soul, life after death, and so on. Politically, the Marxian state he advocated is one where property rights ... and virtually all rights ... disappear in favor of an all-powerful central government."

In the Washington Times, January 1984, Senator Jeremiah Denton, who heads the Senate Subcommittee on Terrorism, stated:

"Liberation theologians have expropriated traditional Christian beliefs and doctrines, added a strong dose of Cuban-style Marxist teaching, and produced an effective but camouflaged army of religious-cum-revolutionaries." Further he stated, "to the liberation theologian the gospel means establishing a messianic solidarity with the oppressed and providing active assistance to all forms of class struggle."

Jesus Christ is God's gift to all the world , both the rich and the poor...God does not discriminate. We may find ourselves joining sides, literally becoming a front for the anti-Christ powers to gain strength using the Christian sympathizers to influence our Christian democratic form of government, creating confusion and weakening our structure to the benefit of the Communist.

We have a definite responsibility to pray for and uphold the government we live under. Every American citizen is a part of our American government. Every citizen makes up the U.S. Government by virtue of his right to vote. Your involvement or lack of it will not excuse you from God's divine judgement upon our nation for its evil unGodly actions. We should think more highly of our own country than any other, if we are going to be an example to the rest of the world. We should be patriotic, however keeping that in balance with the Kingdom of God... remember, we are both secular (natural) and spiritual (the church).

We need more Christians running for elected office. We can change the world by encouraging born-again leadership and giving our own legislators regular input. Find out who your local senators and representatives are, and have their addresses and phone numbers handy. Be informed on the issues. Write letters or call, because they are strongly influenced by the response they receive from their constituents. It often takes very little to change laws and rules in our country. Remember, a single woman, Madalyn Murray O'Hair, initiated the expulsion of prayer in our public schools.

CHAPTER 18

How Much Good Can One Person Do By Voting?

When I go to the polls and cast my single vote, I realize that my vote is just one of many, but somehow I get a satisfaction deep inside that I have done my God-given duty and responsibility.

I feel that I have done what God wants me to do for His sake, and for the sake of this world and for my family's sake. For the person who wonders about the value of one simple vote, let's be reminded that elections have been won or lost by a single vote. If everyone would think, ''My vote won't count, so why vote?'', we would not have the system that we have enjoyed in the United States for over 200 years. It is the individual vote that makes the total system work.

A person who does not participate in the election process by voting certainly has no right to complain about the actions of elected government officials.

I personally believe every Christian in America should be interested in who his lawmakers and policy formers are and get involved to insure that our future includes God. Godly people can be chosen to represent our faith in God, not only for this generation but also for future generations. I believe we are responsible. Christian statesman Edmund Burke said it well: ''The only thing necessary for the triumph of evil is for good men to do nothing.''

CHAPTER 19

How Should One Stay Informed About Political Candidates And Elections?

I think the church should accept the role of alerting Christians to the importance of upcoming elections, in spite of the misguided notion that church and state (political issues) should be kept separate. Though presidential elections are most popular, congressional and senatorial election years can be very critical. Liberal or conservative control of the House of Representatives and the Senate can determine vital issues for the Christian.

I encourage people to send letters and money to the lobbyists for Christian principles and morals. I believe that Christian people should be instructed from the pulpit by their pastors, even though some issues may be termed ''political.'' Too many pastors don't care to become involved and thereby deny their people answers from a Biblical and Christian perspective. I believe God holds us leaders accountable to inform our people to support Godly moral issues such as right-to-life and prayer and Bible reading for our children.

Most people cannot get to Washington, D.C. to speak their views personally. But we can give $10 or $15 in response to some of the appeal letters that we receive. We should read them carefully and pray; then either send a contribution or ignore it, according to what God shows us.

We should find out what the political candidates stand for, ask questions and support with our time and finances those God-fearing Christians who run for office. Church people should take a more active role in lobbying our government for Godly principles, backing up the Word of God. Christians are the God-inspired voices that can influence our world toward God and His Kingdom. Matt. 6:33.

CHAPTER 20

Do You Feel We Are Living In The "Endtimes"?

We're very definitely living in the last days of time. Time had a beginning and time must have an ending, 11 Timothy 3:1. I believe we will see more plaguies, serious earthquakes, more famines, more droughts, and violent storms, because as evil expresses itself, God's Spirit becomes more powerful and more visual. God's Spirit becomes more obvious. God's glory must become manifest. Habakkuk 2:14.

I am convinced that this ''endtime'' generation will see spectacular miracles of God — walking on water, bringing fire out of the heavens, phenomenal healings. God's power will become more obvious as the church gets stronger and stronger; and as the world progessively degenerates. God's children are known as children of light while the unbelieving world reels to and fro in darkness . . . void of truth. Light shines brightest in darkness. John 8:12.

The entire world system is caught in a struggle between God and the devil, i.e. good and evil. Darkness is the absence of light. Truth is light and will untimately triumph.

As God's people take their authority, the devil has to listen. Mankind will resist God, and will thus become more devilish. However, mankind will also submit to God, and become more Godly. Both will happen simultaneously in our society. Listen to God's prophet... ''For behold, the darkness shall cover the earth, and deep darkness the people; but the Lord will arise over you, and His glory will be seen upon you.'' Isaiah 60:2.

Chapter 21

What Do You Mean, That Christians Will Take Their "Authority"?

Christians have not always taken a back seat in dealing with governmental issues. The history of the United States is teeming with Christian leaders who took aggressive, powerful, Godly stands to make our Constitution, Bill of Rights and other foundational ordinances. Every major governmental document was Biblically based. Our forefathers paid a great price for that. They spent many, many hours in prayer and fasting to ensure the freedoms and opportunities for future generations of our great nation.

The church will need to follow suit if we are to see the idealistic changes needed to bring the nation back into that kind of order. I believe the great affluence of our nation resulting from our victory in the Second World War has contributed to our declining interest in Godly standards. We have been "glorying" in the blessings that have come to us — many jobs available, money flowing freely. Some professed Christians are obsessed with the material things of life (II Tim. 3:2-5), causing their minds to ignore the truths and principles of Godliness. The decade of the '50s birthed perhaps the most anti-God philosophies that our country now is reaping.

We at Christian Retreat observe that when our nation is prospering — interest rates lower and inflation down, people have more money to spend, thus less dependency upon God — a Christian facility like ours experience a more difficult time. People's giving decreases and their minds stray from spiritual matters.

However, when our country goes into recession, and the nation as a whole is struggling, people tend to be more interested in the things of God . . . out attendance increases, people get involved, and they give more of what they have to God's work.

We need to take "authority" over our dilemmas and problems, using Godly principles.

CHAPTER 22

Some Christians Believe That The World Cannot Be Saved Or Changed, That All Our Efforts Are In Vain Because God Has A Plan He Has Set In Motion And There Is Nothing We Can Do. Should We Let God Bring This Endtime To A Close As He Is Going To Do Sovereignly?

If I believed and trusted that mentality, I would have to reject the New Testament and Jesus Christ. But I'm a follower of Jesus Christ and Jesus said, "Go ye therefore and teach all nations, baptizing them in the name of the Father, of the Son and of the Holy Ghost, teaching them to observe all the things I have commanded you: and lo I am with you alway, even unto the end of the world. Amen. "We have another mandate from Jesus in Luke 19:13..."Occupy till I come."

Though I live in this secular evil world, Jesus Christ came into my life and that effected a change in me for the good. Now I understand. The Christian errs if he says that the world is going bad anyway, so don't try — wait for "something else" to happen . . . . or wait for a sudden taking-me-out-and-away-to-heaven that will free me from current responsibilities.

Every Christian has a mandate from God to anticipate this

whole world to change. God's Kingdom is coming, even though we know that in the last days the world will burn up with fire, be totally destroyed, and there will be a new heaven and a new earth, 11 Peter 3:10-13. But the Spirit of God in the believer motivates him to bring hope to our world. ''Christ is the answer.''

We must yield to this Christ who has brought hope to us. We must share that same hope with everyone we meet. To think negatively, or to ''give up''   is to be anti-Christ.

Some Christians would suggest that we can go into all the world and preach the Gospel without getting involved in government and politics. That's true if you are merely building up a church and want to implant religion in people's minds. If they want to simply add members to their churches and make their religion compatible with other religions in the world, they don't have to become involved.

But genuine Christianity affects the lives of people in their conscience, convictions and lifestyle. When people are thinking, acting and living differently, so will the political system and lifestyle of the nations be affected!

America's Christian Heritage

by Bill and Nita Scoggan

America's current writers of history textbooks have tried to deny or obscure the fact that our nation was founded upon belief in God. More than that, our forefathers came with a zeal to further the gospel of Jesus Christ in this new undeveloped land.

The faith of the founders of this great nation is very evident in the historical statements which have been documented. The founders never intended a separation of *God* and *State.*

The quotations listed below have been preserved for us and all future generations in scrolls of parchment, on walls and cornerstones of America's historic buildings, on the Liberty Bell, on our coins, and the pages of many books.

These statements reveal their deep faith in God, and an acknowledgement of a total dependency on His divine grace and help to establish this new nation.

It is the responsibility of Christians in America to spread and pass on these *truths* of our Christian heritage to as many people as possible, in order to promote and restore a zeal for righteousness and godliness in our land.

1606—First Charter of Virginia

This charter specified that the Virginia Colony should bring glory to almighty God and advance the Christian faith.

1620—Mayflower Compact

Forty-one Pilgrims prepared the first written constitution of our land. It began: ''In the name of God, Amen. Having undertaken for the Glory of God and advancement of the Christian faith . . . do . . . solemnly and mutually in the presence of God covenant and combine ourselves together . . .''

1620—New England Charter
". . . to advance the enlargement of Christian religion, to the glory of God Almighty."

1622—The Carolinas' Charter
Acknowledged that the settlement was constituted for "the propagation of the Christian faith."

1638—Fundamental Orders of Connecticut
". . . confederation together to maintain and preserve the liberty and purity of the gospel of our Lord Jesus which we now profess."

1643—Constitution of the New England Confederation
"Whereas we all came into these parts of America with one and the same end and aim, namely to advance the kingdom of our Lord Jesus Christ and to enjoy the Liberties of the Gospel in purity with peace."

1681—William Penn (Founder of Pennsylvania, Crusader for religious freedom)
"If you are not governed by God, you will be ruled by tyrants."

1752—Liberty Bell
"Proclaim Liberty throughout the land unto all the inhabitants thereof."   Leviticus 25:10.

1772—Samuel Adams (Patriot, Statesman)
"The rights of the Colonists as Christians . . . may be best understood by reading and carefully studying the institution of the great Law Giver and Head of the Christian Church, which are to be found clearly written and promulgated in the New Testament."

47

1775—The Continental Congress

This body officially called all citizens to fast and pray and confess their sin that God might bless them.

1775—Washington's Cruisers Flag

The flag carries these words: ''An Appeal to Heaven''

1776—Declaration of Independence

Four specific references to the dependence of our nation upon God:

''. . . the laws of Nature and of Nature's God . . .''

''. . . that all men are created equal, that they are endowed by their Creator with certain inalienable rights . . .''

''. . . appealing to the Supreme Judge of the world for the rectitude of our intentions . . .''

''. . . with a firm reliance on the protection of divine Providence . . .''

1776—Chaplains in the Armed Forces

After signing the Declaration of Independence, General Geroge Washington issued an order placing a chaplain in each regiment. They were instructed to have prayers of thanksgiving to Almighty God.

1787—Benjamin Franklin (Statesman, Diplomat, Scientist, Inventor)

Franklin helped draft the Declaration of Independence and was the only man who signed all four of the following documents: The Declaration of Independence, the Treaty of Alliance with France, the Treaty of Paris ending the Revolution, and the Constitution.

''Here is my creed, I believe in one God, the creator of the Universe. That he governs it by his Providence. That he ought to be worshipped.''

At the Constitutional Convention: ''I have lived, Sir, a long time, and the longer I live, the more convincing proofs I see of this truth . . . that God governs in the affairs of men. And if a sparrow cannot fall to the ground without His notice, is it probable that an empire can rise without his aid?'' Franklin went on to call for prayer at the beginning of each session.

1787—Alexander Hamilton (America's 1st Secretary of the Treasury)

Soon after the Constitutional Convention: ''For my own part, I sincerely esteem it a system which without the finger of God, never could have been suggested and agreed upon by such a diversity of interests.''

1789—George Washington—Thanksgiving Day Proclamation

''Whereas it is the duty of all nations to acknowledge the providence of Almighty God, to obey His will, to be grateful for His benefits, and humbly to implore His protection, aid and favors . . . Now, therefore, do I assign and recommend Thursday, the 26th day of November next . . . that we may then all unite in rendering unto Him our sincere and humble thanks for His kind care and protection of the people of this country, and for all the great and various favors which He has been pleased to confer upon us.''

1789—George Washington—The Inaugural Address (America's 1st President)

Every President since Washington has included in his inaugural address reference to his and the nation's dependence upon God.

1820—Daniel Webster

(Plymouth, Mass.)''. . . More than all, a government and a country were to commence, with the very first foundations laid under the divine light of the Christian religion. . . Who would wish that his country's existence had otherwise begun?''
''Let us not forget the religious character of our origin.''

July 4, 1821—John Quincy Adams (America's 6th President)

"From the day of the Declaration . . . they (the American people) were bound by the laws of God, which they all, and by the laws of the Gospel, which they nearly all, acknowledged as the rules of their conduct."

1861—Abraham Lincoln (America's 16th President)

Farewell words in Springfield, Illinois, February 11: "Unless the great God who assisted him (Washington) shall be with me and aid me, I must fail; but if the same omniscient mind and almighty arm that directed and protected him shall guide and support me, I shall not fail—I shall succeed. Let us pray that the God of our fathers may not forsake us now."

1863—Abraham Lincoln—The Gettysburg Address

". . . that this nation, under God, shall have a new birth of freedom and that government of the people, by the people, and for the people shall not perish from the earth."

1863—Abraham Lincoln—National Day of Fasting and Prayer Proclamation

". . . it is the duty of nations,tas well as of men, to owe their independence upon the overruling power of God, to confess their sins and transgressions, in humble sorry, yet with assured hope that genuine repentance will lead to mercy and pardon, and to recognize the sublime truth, announced in the Holy Scriptures and proven by all history, that *those nations only are blessed whose God is the Lord . . .*"

". . . We have been the recipients of the choicest bounties of Heaven. We have been preserved these many years in peace and prosperity. We have grown in numbers, wealth, and power as no other nation has ever grown. But we have forgotten God . . . Intoxicated with unbroken success, we have become . . . too proud to pray to the God that made us!"

" . . . I hereby request all the People to abstain on that day from their ordinary secular pursuits, and to unite, at their several places of public worship and in their respective homes, in keeping the day holy to the Lord . . .

"All this being done, in sincerity and truth, let us then rest humbly in the hope, authorized by the Divine teachings, that the united cry of the Nation will be heard on high, and answered with blessings, no less than the pardon of our national sins . . ."

1863—Motto On Coins

Secretary of the Treasury, Salmon P. Chase instructed the U.S. mint to begin inscribing "In God We Trust" on all coins.

1892—U.S. Supreme Court

Supreme Court Justice Brewer, delivering the opinion of the Court stated: "These, and many other matters which might be noticed, add a volume of unofficial declarations to the mass of organic utterances—that this is a Christian nation."

July 4, 1913—Woodrow Wilson (America's 28th President)

"Here is the nation God has builded by our hands."

March 3, 1931—National Anthem Adopted by Congress

The Star Spangled Banner closes: "Praise the Power that hath made and preserved us a nation. Then conquer we must, when our cause it is just. And this be our motto—'In God is our Trust'."

June 14, 1954—Pledge of Allegiance

Words "under God" adopted by Congress. "I pledge allegiance to the flag of the United States of America, and to the Republic for which it stands, one nation, under God, indivisible, with liberty and justice for all."

June 20, 1956—National Motto

A joint Resolution was passed by Congress, establishing "In God We Trust" as the national motto of the United States of America.

Other historical declarations of faith:

The Prayer Room in the U.S. Capital Building: located under the rotunda for use by those serving in Congress. A large open Bible lies on the alter facing a stained glass window showing George Washington in prayer.

Jefferson Memorial, Washington, D.C.: Inscribed on the wall is Thomas Jefferson's warning: "God who gave us life gave us liberty. Can the liberties of a nation be secure when we have removed a conviction that these liberties are the gift of God?"

All 50 State Constitutions: All contain a statement of faith recognizing dependence upon Almighty God. Together they become the expression of faith of the American people.

Share these truths at every opportunity.

* Reprinted by permission from
America, Wake Up, by Bill and Nita Scoggan, published by Royalty Pubishing Co., P.O. Box 2016, Manassas, Va. 22110 ($5.95) Obtain copies from Publishers or Christian Retreat, Rt. 2, Box 279, Bradenton, Fl 34202.

The Constitution

OF THE
UNITED STATES
OF AMERICA

We the People of the United States, in Order to form
a more perfect Union, establish Justice, insure domestic
Tranquility, provide for the common defence, promote the
general Welfare, and secure the Blessings of Liberty to ourselves
and our Posterity, do ordain and establish this Constitution for
the United States of America.

ARTICLE I.

SECTION 1. All legislative Powers herein granted shall be
vested in a Congress of the United States, which shall consist of a
Senate and House of Representatives.

SECTION 2. The House of Representatives shall be composed
of Members chosen every second Year by the People of the
several States, and the Electors in each State shall have the
Qualifications requisite for Electors of the most numerous Branch
of the State Legislature.

No Person shall be a Representative who shall not have attained to the Age of twenty-five Years, and been seven Years a
Citizen of the United States, and who shall not, when elected, be
an Inhabitant of the State in which he shall be chosen.

(Representatives and direct Taxes shall be apportioned among the several States which may be included within this Union, according to their respective Numbers, which shall be determined be adding to the whole Number of free Persons, including those bound to Service for a Term of Years, and excluding Indians not taxed, three fifths of all other Persons.)* The actual Enumeration shall be made within three Years after the first Meeting of the Congress of the United States, and within every subsequent Term of ten Years, in such Manner as they shall by Law direct. The Number of Representatives shall not exceed one for every thirty Thousand,** but each State shall have at Least one Representative; and until such enumeration shall be made, the State of New Hampshire shall be entitled to chuse three, Massachusetts eight, Rhode-Island and Providence Plantations one, Connecticut five, New-York six, New Jersey four, Pennsylvania eight, Delaware one, Maryland six, Virginia ten, North Carolina five, South Carolina five, and Georgia three.

(Note: This booklet presents the Constitution and all amendments in their original form. Items which have since been amended or superseded, as identified in the footnotes, are bracketed.)

When vacancies happen in the representation from any State, the Executive Authority thereof shall issue Writs of Election to fill such Vacancies.

The House of Representatives shall chuse their Speaker and other Officers; and shall have the sole Power of Impeachment.

SECTION 3. The Senate of the United States shall be composed of two Senators from each State, (chosen by the Legislature thereof ,)*** for six Years; and each Senator shall have one Vote.

Immediately after they shall be assembled in Consequence of the first Election, they shall be divided as equally as may be into three Classes. The Seats of the Senators of the first Class shall be vacated at the Expiration of the second Year, of the second Class at the Expiration of the fourth Year, and of the third Class at the

*Changed by section 2 of the fourteenth amendment.
**Ratio in 1965 was one to over 410,000.
***Changed by section 1 of the seventeenth amendment.

Expiration of the sixth Year, so that one-third may be chosen every second year; (and if Vacancies happen by Resignation, or otherwise, during the Recess of the Legislature of any State, the Executive thereof may make temporary Appointments until the next Meeting of the Legislature, which shall then fill such Vacancies.)*

No Person shall be a Senator who shall not have attained to the Age of thirty Years, and been nine Years a Citizen of the United States, and who shall not, when elected, be an Inhabitant of that State from which he shall be chosen.

The Vice President of the United States shall be President of the Senate, but shall have no Vote, unless they be equally divided.

The Senate shall chuse their other Officers, and also a President pro tempore, in the absence of the Vice President, or when he shall exercise the Office of President of the United States.

The Senate shall have the sole Power to try all Impeachments. When sitting for that Purpose, they shall be on Oath or Affirmation. When the President of the United States is tried, the Chief Justice shall preside: And no Person shall be convicted without the Concurrence of two thirds of the Members present.

Judgment in Cases of Impeachment shall not extend further than to removal from Office, and disqualification to hold and enjoy any Office of honor, Trust or Profit under the United States: but the Party convicted shall nevertheless be liable and subject to Indictment, Trial, Judgment and Punishment, according to Law.

SECTION 4. The Times, Places and Manner of holding Elections for Senators and Representatives, shall be prescribed in each State by the Legislature thereof; but the Congress may at any time by Law make or alter such Regulations, except as to the Place of Chusing Senators.

*Changed by clause 2 of the seventeenth amendment.

The Congress shall assemble at least once in every Year, and such Meeting shall be on the first Monday in December,ı»» unless they shall by Law appoint a different Day.

SECTION 5. Each House shall be the Judge of the Elections, Returns and Qualifications of its own Members, and a Majority of each shall constitute a Quorum to do Business; but a smaller number may adjourn from day to day, and may be authorized to compel the Attendance of absent Members, in such Manner, and under such Penalties as each House may provide.

Each House may determine the Rules of its Proceedings, punish its Members for disorderly Behavior, and, with the Concurrence of two thirds, expel a Member.

Each House shall keep a Journal of its Proceedings, and from time to time publish the same, excepting such Parts as may in their Judgment require Secrecy; and the Yeas and Nays of the Members of either House on any question shall, at the Desire of one fifth of those Present, be entered on the Journal.

Neither House, during the Session of Congress, shall, without the Consent of the other, adjourn for more than three days, nor to any other Place than that in which the two Houses shall be sitting.

SECTION 6. The Senators and Representatives shall receive a Compensation for their Services, to be ascertained by Law, and paid out of the Treasury of the United States. They shall in all Cases, except Treason, Felony and Breach of the Peace, be privileged from Arrest during their Attendance at the Session of their respective Houses, and in going to and returning from the same; and for any Speech or Debate in either House, they shall not be questioned in any other Place.

**Changed by section 2 of the twentieth amendment.

No Senator or Representative shall, during the Time for which he was elected, be appointed to any civil Office under the Authority of the United States, which shall have been created, or the Emoluments whereof shall have been encreased during such time; and no Person holding any Office under the United States, shall be a Member of either House during his Continuance in Office.

SECTION 7. All Bills for raising Revenue shall originate in the House of Representatives; but the Senate may propose or concur with Amendments as on other Bills.

Every Bill which shall have passed the House of Representatives and the Senate, shall, before it become a Law, be presented to the President of the United States; If he approve he shall sign it, but if not he shall return it, with his Objections to that House in which it shall have originated, who shall enter the Objections at large on their Journal, and proceed to reconsider it. If after such Reconsideration two thirds of that House shall agree to pass the Bill, it shall be sent, together with the Objections, to the other House, by which it shall likewise be reconsidered, and if approved by two thirds of that House, it shall become a Law. But in all such Cases the Votes of both Houses shall be determined by Yeas and Nays, and the Names of the Persons voting for and against the Bill shall be entered on the Journal of each House respectively. If any Bill shall not be returned by the President within ten Days (Sundays excepted) after it shall have been presented to him, the Same shall be a Law, in like Manner as if he had signed it, unless the Congress by their Adjournment prevent its Return, in which Case it shall not be a Law.

Every Order, Resolution, or Vote to which the Concurrence of the Senate and House of Representatives may be necessary (except on a question of Adjournment) shall be presented to the President of the United States; and before the Same shall take Effect, shall be approved by him, or being disapproved by him, shall be repassed by two thirds of the Senate and House of Representatives, according to the Rules and Limitations prescribed in the Case of a Bill.

SECTION 8. The Congress shall have Power To lay and collect Taxes, Duties, Imposts and Excises, to pay the Debts and provide for the common Defence and general Welfare of the United States; but all Duties, Imposts and Excises shall be uniform throughout the United States;

To borrow money on the credit of the United States;

To regulate Commerce with foreign Nations, and among the several States, and with the Indian Tribes;

To establish an uniform Rule of Naturalization, and uniform Laws on the subject of Bankruptcies throughout the United States;

To coin Money, regulate the Value thereof, and of foreign Coin, and fix the Standard of Weights and Measures;

To provide for the Punishment of counterfeiting the Securities and current Coin of the United States;

To establish Post Offices and post Roads;

To promote the Progress of Science and useful Arts, by securing for limited Times to Authors and Inventors the exclusive Right to their respective Writings and Discoveries;

To constitute Tribunals inferior to the supreme Court;

To define and punish Piracies and Felonies committed on the high Seas, and Offenses against the Law of Nations;

To declare War, grant Letters of Marque and Reprisal, and make Rules concerning Captures on Land and Water;

To raise and support Armies, but no Appropriation of Money to that Use shall be for a longer Term than two Years;

To provide and maintain a Navy;

To make Rules for the Government and Regulation of the land and naval Forces;

To provide for calling forth the Militia to execute the Laws of the Union, suppress Insurrections and repel Invasions;

To provide for organizing, arming, and disciplining the Militia, and for governing such Part of them as may be employed in the Service of the United States, reserving to the States respectively, the Appointment of the Officers, and the Authority of training the Militia according to the discipline prescribed by Congress;

To exercise exclusive Legislation in all Cases whatsoever, over such District (not exceeding ten Miles square) as may, by Cession of particular States, and the acceptance of Congress, become the Seat of the Government of the United States, and to exercise like Authority over all Places purchased by the Consent of the Legislature of the State in which the Same shall be, for the Erection of Forts, Magazines, Arsenals, dock-Yards, and other needful Buildings;—And

To make all Laws which shall be necessary and proper for carrying into Execution the foregoing Powers, and all other Powers vested by this Constitution in the Government of the United States, or in any Department or Officer thereof.

SECTION 9. The Migration or Importation of such Persons as any of the States now existing shall think proper to admit, shall not be prohibited by the Congress prior to the Year one thousand eight hundred and eight, but a tax or duty may be imposed on such Importation, not exceeding ten dollars for each Person.

The privilege of the Writ of Habeas Corpus shall not be suspended, unless when in Cases of Rebellion or Invasion the public Safety may require it.

No Bill of Attainder or ex post facto Law shall be passed.

No capitation, or other direct, Tax shall be laid, unless in Proportion to the Census or Enumeration herein before directed to be taken. *

No Tax or Duty shall be laid on Articles exported from any State.

*But see the sixteenth amendment.

60

No Preference shall be given by any Regulation of Commerce or Revenue to the Ports of one State over those of another; nor shall Vessels bound to, or from, one State, be obliged to enter, clear, or pay Duties to another.

No Money shall be drawn from the Treasury, but in Consequence of Appropriations made by Law; and a regular Statement and Account of the Receipts and Expenditures of all public Money shall be published from time to time.

No Title of Nobility shall be granted by the United States; And, no Person holding any Office of Profit or Trust under them, shall, without the Consent of the Congress, accept of any present, Emolument, Office, or Title, of any kind whatever, from any King, Prince, or foreign State.

SECTION 10. No State shall enter into any Treaty, Alliance, or Confederation; grant Letters of Marque and Reprisal; coin Money; emit Bills of Credit; make any Thing but gold and silver Coin a Tender in Payment of Debts; pass any Bill of Attainder, ex post facto Law, or Law impairing the Obligation of Contracts, or grant any Title of Nobility.

No State shall, without the Consent of the Congress, lay any Imposts or Duties on Imports or Exports, except what may be absolutely necessary for executing its inspection Laws: and the net Produce of all Duties and Imposts, laid by any State on Imports or Exports, shall be for the Use of the Treasury of the United States; and all such Laws shall be subject to the Revision and Controul of the Congress.

No State shall, without the Consent of Congress, lay any duty of Tonnage, keep Troops, or Ships of War in time of Peace, enter into any Agreement or Compact with another State, or with a foreign Power, or engage in War, unless actually invaded, or in such imminent Danger as will not admit of delay.

ARTICLE II.

SECTION 1. The executive Power shall be vested in a President of the United States of America. He shall hold his Office during the Term of four Years, and, together with the Vice-President, chosen for the same Term, be elected, as follows.

Each State shall appoint, in such Manner as the Legislature thereof may direct, a Number of Electors, equal to the whole Number of Senators and Representatives to which the State may be entitled in the Congress; but no Senator or Representative, or Person holding an Office of Trust or Profit under the United States, shall be appointed an Elector.

(The Electors shall meet in their respective States, and vote by Ballot for two persons, of whom one at least shall not be an Inhabitant of the same State with themselves. And they shall make a List of all the Persons voted for, and of the Number of Votes for each; which List they shall sign and certify, and transmit sealed to the Seat of the Government of the United States, directed to the President of the Senate. The President of the Senate shall, in the Presence of the Senate and House of Representatives, open all the Certificates, and the Votes shall then be counted. The Person having the greatest Number of Votes shall be the President, if such Number be a Majority of the whole Number of Electors appointed; and if there be more than one who have such Majority, and have an equal Number of Votes, then the House of Representatives shall immediately chuse by Ballot one of them for President; and if no Person have a Majority, then from the five highest on the List the said House shall in like Manner chuse the President. But in chusing the President, the Votes shall be taken by States, the Representation from each State having one Vote; a quorum for this Purpose shall consist of a Member or Members from two thirds of the States, and a Majority of all the States shall be necessary to a Choice. In every Case, after the Choice of the President, the Person having the greatest Number of Votes of the Electors shall be the Vice President. But if there should remain two or more who have equal Votes, the Senate shall chuse from them by Ballot the Vice-President.)*

The Congress may determine the Time of chusing the Electors, and the Day on which they shall give their Votes; which Day shall be the same throughout the United States.

No person except a natural born Citizen, or a Citizen of the United States, at the time of the Adoption of this Constitution, shall be eligible to the Office of President; neither shall any Person be eligible to that Office who shall not have attained to the Age of thirty-five Years, and been fourteen Years a Resident within the United States.

**(In Case of the Removal of the President from Office, or of his Death, Resignation, or Inability to discharge the Powers and Duties of the said Office, the same shall devolve on the Vice President, and the Congress may by Law, provide for the Case of Removal, Death, Resignation or Inability, both of the President and Vice President, declaring what Officer shall then act as President, and such Officer shall act accordingly, until the Disability be removed, or a President shall be elected.)

The President shall, at stated Times, receive for his Services, a Compensation, which shall neither be increased nor diminished during the Period for which he shall have been elected, and he shall not receive within that Period any other Emolument from the United States, or any of them.

Before he enter on the Execution of his Office, he shall take the following Oath or Affirmation:—''I do solemnly swear (or affirm) that I will faithfully execute the Office of the President of the United States, and will to the best of my Ability, preserve, protect and defend the Constitution of the United States.''

*Superseded by the twelfth amendment.
**This clause has been affected by the twenty-fifth amendment.

SECTION 2. The President shall be Commander in Chief of the Army and Navy of the United States, and of the Militia of the several States, when called into the actual Service of the United States; he may require the Opinion in writing, of the principal Officer in each of the executive Departments, upon any subject relating to the Duties of their respective Offices, and he shall have Power to Grant Reprieves and Pardons for Offenses against the United States, except in Cases of Impeachment.

He shall have Power, by and with the Advice and Consent of the Senate, to make Treaties, provided two-thirds of the Senators present concur; and he shall nominate, and by and with the Advice and Consent of the Senate, shall appoint Ambassadors, other public Ministers and Consuls, Judges of the supreme Court, and all other Officers of the United States, whose Appointments are not herein otherwise provided for, and which shall be established by Law; but the Congress may by Law vest the Appointment of such inferior Officers, as they think proper, in the President alone, in the Courts of Law, or in the Heads of Departments.

The President shall have Power to fill up all Vacancies that may happen during the Recess of the Senate, by granting Commissions which shall expire at the End of their next Session.

SECTION 3. He shall from time to time give to the Congress Information of the State of the Union, and recommend to their Consideration such Measures as he shall judge necessary and expedient; he may, on extraordinary Occasions, convene both Houses, or either of them, and in Case of Disagreement between them, with Respect to the Time of Adjournment, he may adjourn them to such Time as he shall think proper; he shall receive Ambassadors and other public Ministers; he shall take Care that the Laws be faithfully executed, and shall Commission all the Officers of the United States.

SECTION 4. The President, Vice President and all civil Officers of the United States, shall be removed from Office on Impeachment for, and Conviction of, Treason, Bribery, or other high Crimes and Misdemeanors.

ARTICLE III.

SECTION 1. The judical Power of the United States, shall be vested in one supreme Court, and in such inferior Courts as the

Congress may from time to time ordain and establish. The Judges, both of the supreme and inferior Courts, shall hold their Offices during good Behaviour, and shall, at stated Times, receive for their Services, a Compensation, which shall not be diminished during their Continuance in Office.

SECTION 2. The judical Power shall extend to all Cases, in Law and Equity, arising under this Constitution, the Laws of the United States, and Treaties made, or which shall be made, under their Authority;—to all Cases affecting Ambassadors, other public Ministers and Consuls;—to all Cases of admiralty and maritime Jurisdiction;—to Controversies to which the United States shall be a Party;—to Controversies between two or more States;—between a State and Citizens of another State;—between Citizens of different States;—between Citizens of the same State claiming Lands under Grants of different States, and between a State, or the Citizens thereof, and foreign States, Citizens or Subjects.

In all Cases affecting Ambassadors, other public Ministers and Consuls, and those in which a State shall be Party, the supreme Court shall have original Jurisdiction. In all the other Cases before mentioned, the supreme Court shall have appellate Jurisdiction, both as to Law and Fact, with such Exceptions, and under such Regulations as the Congress shall make.

The trial of all Crimes, except in Cases of Impreachment, shall be by Jury; and such Trial shall be held in the State where the said Crimes shall have been committed; but when not committed within any State, the Trial shall be at such Place or Places as the Congress may by Law have directed.

SECTION 3. Treason against the United States, shall consist only in levying War against them, or in adhering to their Enemies, giving them Aid and Comfort. No Person shall be convicted of Treason unless on the Testimony of two Witnesses to the same overt Act, or on Confession in open Court.

The Congress shall have Power to declare the Punishment of Treason, but no Attainder of Treason shall work Corruption of

Blood, or Forfeiture except during the Life of the Person attainted.

ARTICLE IV.

SECTION 1. Full Faith and Credit shall be given in each State to the public Acts, Records, and judical Proceedings of every other State. And the Congress may by general Laws prescribe the Manner in which such Acts, Records and Proceedings shall be proved, and the Effect thereof.

SECTION 2. The Citizens of each State shall be entitled to all Privileges and Immunities of Citizens in the several States.

A Person charged in any State with Treason, Felony, or other Crime, who shall flee from Justice, and be found in another State, shall on demand of the executive Authority of the State from which he fled, be delivered up, to be removed to the State having Jurisdiction of the Crime.

(No Person held to Service or Labour in one State, under the Laws thereof, escaping into another, shall, in Consequence of any Law or Regulation therein, be discharged from such Service or Labour, but shall be delivered up on Claim of the Party to whom such Service or Labour may be due.)*

SECTION 3. New States may be admitted by the Congress into this Union; but no new State shall be formed or erected within the Jurisdiction of any other State; nor any State be formed by the Junction of two or more States, or parts of States, without the Consent of the Legislatures of the States concerned as well as of the Congress.

The Congress shall have Power to dispose of and make all needful Rules and Regulations respecting the Territory or other Property belonging to the United States; and nothing in this Constitution shall be so construed as to Prejudice any Claims of the United States, or of any particular State.

SECTION 4. The United States shall guarantee to every State in this Union a Republican Form of Government, and shall protect each of them against Invasion; and on Application of the

Legislature, or of the Executive (when the Legislature cannot be convened) against domestic Violence.

ARTICLE V.

The Congress, whenever two-thirds of both Houses shall deem it necessary, shall propose Amendments to this Constitution, or, on the Application of the Legislature of two-thirds of the several States, shall call a Convention for proposing Amendments, which, in either Case, shall be valid to all Intents and Purposes, as part of this Constitution, when ratifed by the Legislatures of three-fourths of the several States, or by Conventions in three-fourth thereof, as the one or the other Mode of Ratification may be proposed by the Congress; Provided that no Amendment which may be made prior to the Year One thousand eight hundred and eight shall in any Manner affect the first and fourth Clauses in the Ninth Section of the first Article; and that no State, without its Consent, shall be deprived of its equal Suffrage in the Senate.

ARTICLE VI.

All Debts contracted and Engagements entered into, before the Adoption of this Constitution, shall be as valid against the United States under this Constitution, as under the Confederation.

This Constitution, and the Laws of the United States which shall be made in Pursuance thereof; and all Treaties made, or which shall be made, under the Authority of the United States, shall be the supreme Law of the Land; and the Judges in every State shall be bound thereby, any Thing in the Constitution or Laws of any State to the Contrary notwithstanding.

The Senators and Representatives before mentioned, and the Members of the several State Legislatures, and all executive and judicial Officers, both of the United States and of the several States, shall be bound by Oath or Affirmation, to support this

Constitution; but no religious Test shall ever be required as a Qualification to any Office or public Trust under the United States.

ARTICLE VII.

The Ratification of the Conventions of nine States shall be sufficient for the Establishment of this Constitution between the States so ratifying the Same.

Done in Convention by the Unanimous Consent of the States present the Seventeenth Day of September in the Year of our Lord one thousand seven hundred and Eighty seven and of the Independence of the United States of America the Twelfth. In Witness whereof We have hereunto subscribed our Names.

Go WASHINGTON
Presidt and deputy from Virginia

New Hampshire
John Langdon
Nicholas Gilman

Massachusetts
Nathaniel Gorham
Rufus King

New Jersey
Wil: Livingston
David Brearley
Wm. Paterson
Jona: Dayton

Pennsylvania
B. Franklin
Robt. Morris
Thos. FitzSimons
James Wilson
Thomas Mifflin
Geo. Clymer
Jared Ingersoll
Gouv Morris

Delaware.
Geo: Read
John Dickinson
Jaco: Broom
Gunning Bedford jun
Richard Bassett

Connecticut
Wm. Saml Johnson
Roger Sherman

New York
Alexander Hamilton

Maryland
James McHenry
Danl Carrol
Dan: of St Thos Jenifer

Virginia
John Blair
James Madison Jr.

North Carolina
Wm. Blount
Hu Williamson
Richd Dobbs Spaight.

South Carolina
J. Rutledge
Charles Pinckney
Charles Cotesworth
Pinckney
Pierce Butler

Georgia.
William Few
Abr Baldwin

Attest:

WILLIAM JACKSON, *Secretary.*

ARTICLES IN ADDITION TO, AND AMENDMENT OF, THE CONSTITUTION OF THE UNITED STATES OF AMERICA, PROPOSED BY CONGRESS, AND RATIFIED BY THE LEGISLATURES OF THE SEVERAL STATES, PURSUANT TO THE FIFTH ARTICLE OF THE ORIGINAL CONSTITUTION.*

(The first 10 Amendments were ratified December 15, 1791, and form what is known as the "Bill of Rights")

AMENDMENT I

Congress shall make no law respecting an establishment of religion, or prohibiting the free exercise thereof; or abridging the freedom of speech, or of the press; or the right of the people peaceably to assemble, and to petition the Government for a redress of grievances.

AMENDMENT II

A well regulated Militia, being necessary to the security of a free State, the right of the people to keep and bear Arms, shall not be infringed.

AMENDMENT III

No Soldier shall, in time of peace be quartered in any house, without the consent of the Owner, nor in time of war, but in a manner to be prescribed by law.

---

*Amendment XXI was not ratified by state legislatures, but by state conventions summoned by Congress.

AMENDMENT IV

The right of the people to be secure in their persons, houses, papers, and effects, against unreasonable searches and seizures, shall not be violated, and no Warrants shall issue, but upon probable cause, supported by Oath or affirmation and particularly describing the place to be searched, and the persons or things to be seized.

AMENDMENT V

No person shall be held to answer for a capital, or otherwise infamous crime, unless on a presentment or indictment of a Grand Jury, except in cases arising in the land or naval forces, or in the Militia, when in actual service in time of War or public danger; nor shall any person be subject for the same offence to be twice put in jeopardy of life or limb; nor shall be compelled in any criminal case to be a witness against himself, nor be deprived of life, liberty, or property, without due process of law; nor shall private property be taken for public use, without just compensation.

AMENDMENT VI

In all criminal prosecutions, the accused shall enjoy the right to a speedy and public trial, by an impartial jury of the State and district wherein the crime shall have been committed, which district shall have been previously ascertained by law, and to be informed of the nature and cause of the accusation; to be confronted with the witnesses against him; to have compulsory process for obtaining witnesses in his favor, and to have the Assistance of Counsel for his defence.

AMENDMENT VII

In suits at common law, where the value in controversy shall exceed twenty dollars, the right of trial by jury shall be preserved, and no fact tried by a jury, shall be otherwise reexamined in any Court of the United States, than according to the rules of the common law.

AMENDMENT VIII

Excessive bail shall not be required, nor excessive fines imposed, nor cruel and unusual punishments inflicted.

AMENDMENT IX

The enumeration in the Constitution, of certain rights, shall not be construed to deny or disparage others retained by the people.

AMENDMENT X

The powers not delegated to the United States by the Constitution, nor prohibited by it to the States, are reserved to the States respectively, or to the people.

AMENDMENT XI
(Ratified February 7, 1795)

The Judical power of the United States shall not be construed to extend to any suit in law or equity, commenced or prosecuted against one of the United States by Citizens of another State, or by Citizens or Subjects of any Foreign State.

AMENDMENT XII
(Ratified June 15, 1804)

The Electors shall meet in their respective states and vote by ballot for President and Vice-President, one of whom, at least, shall not be inhabitant of the same state with themselves; they shall name in their ballots the person voted for as President, and in distinct ballots the person voted for as Vice-President, and they shall make distinct lists of all persons voted for as President, and of all persons voted for as Vice-President, and of the number of votes for each, which lists they shall sign and certify, and transmit sealed to the seat of the government of the United States, directed to the President of the Senate;—The President of the Senate shall, in presence of the Senate and House of Representatives, open all the certificates and the votes shall then be counted;—The person having the greatest number of votes for President, shall be the President, if such number be a majority of the whole number of Electors appointed; and if no person have such majority, then from the persons having the highest numbers not exceeding three on the list of those voted for as President, the House of Representatives shall choose immediately, by ballot, the President. But in choosing the President, the votes shall be taken by states, the representation from each state having one vote; a quorum for this purpose shall consist of a member or members from two-thirds of the states, and a majority of all the states shall be necessary to a choice. (And if the House of Representatives shall not choose a President whenever the right of choice shall devolve upon them, before the fourth day of March next following, then the Vice-President shall act as President,as in the case of the death or other constitutional disability of the President.—)* The person having the greatest number of votes as Vice-President, shall be the Vice-President, if such number be a majority of the whole number of Electors appointed, and if no person have a majority, then from the two highest numbers on the list, the Senate shall choose the Vice-President; a quorum for the purpose shall consist of two-thirds of the whole number of Senators, and a majority of the whole number shall be necessary to a choice. But no person constitutionally ineligible to the office of President shall be eligible to that of Vice-President of the United States.

*Superseded by section 3 of the twentieth amendment.

AMENDMENT XIII
(Ratified December 6, 1865)

SECTION 1. Neither slavery nor involuntary servitude, except as a punishment for crime whereof the party shall have been duly convicted, shall exist within the United States, or any place subject to their jurisdiction.

SECTION 2. Congress shall have power to enforce this article by appropriate legislation.

AMENDMENT XIV
(Ratified July 9, 1868)

SECTION 1. All persons born or naturalized in the United States, and subject to the jurisdiction thereof, are citizens of the United States and of the State wherein they reside. No State shall make or enforce any law which shall abridge the privileges or immunities of citizens of the United States; nor shall any State deprive any person of life, liberty, or property, without due process of law; nor deny to any person within its jurisdiction the equal protection of the laws.

SECTION 2. Representatives shall be apportioned among the several States according to their respective numbers, counting the whole number of persons in each State, excluding Indians not taxed; But when the right to vote at any election for the choice of electors for President and Vice-President of the United States, Representatives in Congress, the Executive and Judicial officers of a State, or the members of the Legislature thereof, is denied to any of the male inhabitants of such State, being twenty-one years of age,* and citizens of the United States, or in any way abridged, except for participation in rebellion, or other crime, the basis of

---

*Changed by section 1 of the twenty-sixth amendment.

---

representation therein shall be reduced in the proportion which the number of such male citizens shall bear to the whole number of male citizens twenty-one years of age in such State.

SECTION 3. No person shall be a Senator or Representative in Congress, or elector of President and Vice-President, or hold any office, civil or military, under the United States, or under any State, who, having previously taken an oath, as a member of Congress, or as an officer of the United States, or as a member of any State legislature, or as an executive or judicial officer of any State, to support the Constitution of the United States, shall have engaged in insurrection or rebellion against the same, or given aid or comfort to the enemies thereof. But Congress may by a vote of two-thirds of each House, remove such disability.

SECTION 4. The validity of the public debt of the United States, authorized by law, including debts incurred for payment of pensions and bounties for services in suppressing insurrection or rebellion, shall not be questioned. But neither the United States nor any State shall assume or pay any debt or obligation incurred in aid of insurrection or rebellion against the United States, or any claim for the loss or emancipation of any slave; but all such debts, obligations and claims shall be held illegal and void.

SECTION 5. The Congress shall have power to enforce, by appropriate legislation, the provisions of this article.

AMENDMENT XV
(Ratified February 3,1870)

SECTION 1. The right of citizens of the United States to vote shall not be denied or abridged by the United States or by any State on account of race, color, or previous condition of servitude—

SECTION 2. The Congress shall have power to enforce this article by appropriate legislation.

AMENDMENT XVI
(Ratified February 3, 1913)

The Congress shall have power to lay and collect taxes on incomes, from whatever source derived, without apportionment among several States, and without regard to any census or enumeration.

AMENDMENT XVII
(Ratified April 8, 1913)

The Senate of the United States shall be composed of two Senators from each State, elected by the people thereof, for six years; and each Senator shall have one vote. The electors in each State shall have the qualifications requisite for electors of the most numerous branch of the State legislatures.

When vacancies happen in the representation of any State in the Senate, the executive authority of such State shall issue writs of election to fill such vacancies: *Provided,* That the legislature of any State may empower the executive thereof to make temporary appointments until the people fill the vacancies by election as the legislature may direct.

This amendment shall not be so construed as to affect the election or term of any Senator chosen before it becomes valid as part of the Constitution.

AMENDMENT XVIII
(Ratified January 16, 1919)

SECTION 1. After one year from the ratificatiaon of this article the manufacture, sale, or transportation of intoxicating liquors within, the importation thereof into, or the exportation thereof from the United States and all territory subject to the jurisdiction-thereof for beverage purposes is hereby prohibited.

SECTION 2. The Congress and the several States shall have concurrent power to enforce this article by appropriate legislation.

(SECTION 3. This article shall be inoperative unless it shall have been ratified as an amendment to the Constitution by the legislatures of the several States as provided in the Constitution, within seven years from the date of the submission hereof to the States by the Congress.)*

AMENDMENT XIX
(Ratified August 18, 1920)

The right of citizens of the United States to vote shall not be denied or abridged by the United States or by any State on account of sex.

Congress shall have power to enforce this article by appropriate legislation.

AMENDMENT XX
(Ratified January 23, 1933)

SECTION 1. The terms of the President and Vice President shall end at noon on the 20th day of January, and the terms of Senators and Representatives at noon on the 3d day of January, of the years in which such terms would have ended if this article had not been ratified; and the terms of their successors shall then begin.

SECTION 2. The Congress shall assemble at least once in every year, and such meeting shall begin at noon on the 3d day of January, unless they shall by law appoint a different day.

SECTION 3. If, at the time fixed for the beginning of the term of the President, the President elect shall have died, the Vice President elect shall become President. If a President shall not have been chosen before the time fixed for the beginning of his term, or if the President elect shall have failed to qualify, then the Vice President elect shall act as President until a President shall have qualified; and the Congress may by law provide for the case

---

* Repealed by section 1 of the twenty-first amendment.

wherein neither a President elect nor a Vice President elect shall have qualified, declaring who shall then act as President, or the manner in which one who is to act shall be selected, and such person shall act accordingly until a President or Vice President shall have qualified.

SECTION 4. The Congress may by law provide for the case of the death of any of the persons from whom the House of Representatives may choose a President whenever the right of choice shall have devolved upon them, and for the case of the death of any of the persons from whom the Senate may choose a Vice President whenever the right of choice shall have devolved upon them.

SECTION 5. Sections 1 and 2 shall take effect on the 15th day of October following the ratification of this article.

SECTION 6. This article shall be inoperative unless it shall have been ratified as an amendment to the Constitution by the legislatures of three-fourths of the several States within seven years from the date of its submission.

AMENDMENT XXI
(Ratified December 5, 1933)

SECTION 1. The eighteenth article of amendment to the Constitution of the United States is hereby repealed.

SECTION 2. The transportation or importation into any State, Territory, or possession of the United States for delivery or use therein of intoxicating liquors, in violation of the laws thereof, is hereby prohibited.

SECTION 3. This article shall be inoperative unless it shall have been ratified as an amendment to the Constitution by conventions in the several States, as provided in the Constitution, within seven years from the date of the submission hereof to the States by the Congress.

AMENDMENT XXII
(Ratified February 27, 1951)

SECTION 1. No person shall be elected to the office of the President more than twice, and no person who has held the offece of President, or acted as President, for more than two years of a term to which some other person was elected President shall be elected to the office of the President more than once. But this Article shall not apply to any person holding the office of President when this Article was proposed by the Congress, and shall not prevent any person who may be holding the office of President, or acting as President, during the term within which this Article becomes operative from holding the office of President or acting as President during the remainder of such term.

SECTION 2. This article shall be inoperative unless it shall have been ratified as an amendment to the Constitution by the legislatures of three-fourths of the several States within seven years from the date of its submission to the States by the Congress.

AMENDMENT XXIII
(Ratified March 29, 1961)

SECTION 1. The District constituting the seat of Government

of the United States shall appoint in such manner as the Congress may direct:

A number of electors of President and Vice President equal to the whole number of Senators and Representatives in Congress to which the District would be entitled if it were a State, but in no event more than the least populous State; they shall be in addition to those appointed by the States, but they shall be considered, for the purposes of the election of President and Vice President, to be electors appointed by a State; and they shall meet in the District and perform such duties as provided by the twelfth article of amendment.

SECTION 2. The Congress shall have power to enforce this article by appropriate legislation.

AMENDMENT XXIV
(Ratified January 23, 1964)

SECTION 1. The right of citizens of the United States to vote in any primary or other election for President or Vice President, for electors for President or Vice President, for Senator or Representative in Congress, shall not be denied or abridged by the United States or any State by reason of failure to pay any poll tax or other tax.

SECTION 2. The Congress shall have power to enforce this article by appropriate legislation.

AMENDMENT XXV
(Ratified February 10, 1967)

SECTION 1. In case of the removal of the President from office or of his death or resignation, the Vice President shall become President.

SECTION 2. Whenever there is a vacancy in the office of the Vice President, the President shall nominate a Vice President who shall take office upon confirmation by a majority vote of both Houses of Congress.

SECTION 3. Whenever the President transmits to the President pro tempore of the Senate and the Speaker of the House of Representatives his written declaration that he is unable to discharge the powers and duties of his office, and until he transmits to them a written declaration to the contrary, such powers and duties shall be discharged by the Vice President as Acting President.

SECTION 4. Whenever the Vice President and a majority of either the principal officers of the executive departments or of such other body as Congress may by law provide, transmit to the President pro tempore of the Senate and the Speaker of the House of Representatives their written declaration that the President is unable to discharge the powers and duties of his office, the Vice President shall immediately assume the powers and duties of the office as Acting President.

Thereafter, when the President transmits to the President pro tempore of the Senate and the Speaker of the House of Representatives his written declaration that no inability exists, he shall resume the powers and duties of his office unless the Vice President and a majority of either the principal officers of the executive department or of such other body as Congress may by law provide, transmit within four days to the President pro tempore of the Senate and the Sperker of the House of Representatives their written declaration that the President is unable to discharge the powers and duties of his office. Thereupon Congress shall decide the issue, assembling within forty-eight hours for that purpose if not in session. If the Congress, within twenty-one days after receipt of the latter written declaration, or, if Congress is not in session, within twenty-one days after Congress is required to assemble, determines by two-thirds vote of both Houses that the President is unable to discharge the powers and duties of his office, the Vice President shall continue to discharge the same as Acting President; otherwise, the President shall resume the powers and duties of his office.

AMENDMENT XXVI
(Ratified July 1, 1971)

SECTION 1. The right of citizens of the United States, who are eighteen years of age or older, to vote shall not be denied or abridged by the United States or by any State on account of age.

SECTION 2. The Congress shall have power to enforce this article by appropriate legislation.